Turn to the le[ft]
turn to the ri[ght]

Jack Beers
Illustrations by Mike Hortens

Longman

Edinburgh Gate
Harlow, Essex

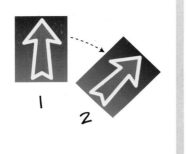

The arrow on the card
points straight up.
If I turn the card a little,
the arrow points
in a different direction.

Now I turn the card
a little more.
See where the arrow
points now.
This is the end
of a quarter turn
to the right.

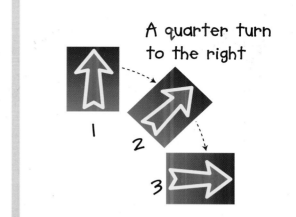

A quarter turn
to the right

1

2

3

If I turn this card to the right,
the snowman turns to the right, too.

I keep turning the card
to the right.
Which way does
the snowman turn?
Which card comes next, a or b?
This is the end of a quarter turn
to the right.

A quarter turn
to the right

a.

b.

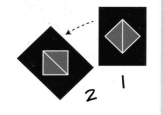

If I turn this card to the left,
the square turns to the left, too.

I keep turning the card to the left. Which card comes next, a or b? This is the end of a quarter turn to the left.

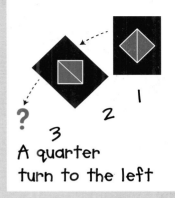

A quarter turn to the left

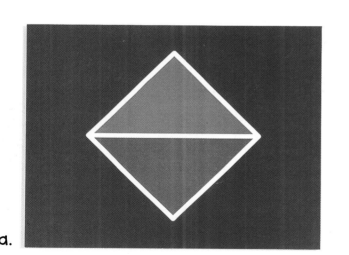

a.

b.

I turn this card
a quarter turn to the right.

Which card comes next, a or b?

a.

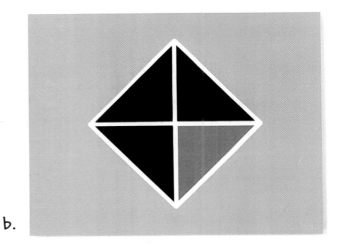

b.

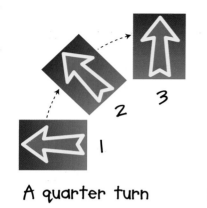

A quarter turn

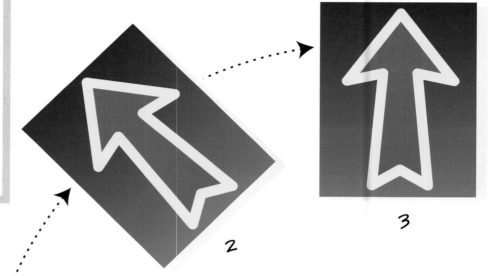

I turn this card
even further.
This turn is called
a half turn.

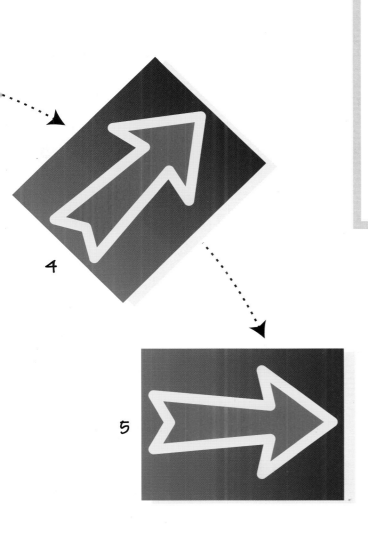

4

5

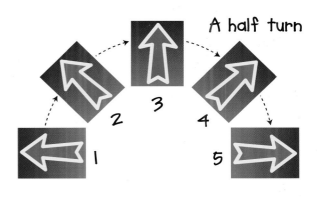

A half turn

2 3 4

1 5

At the end
of the turn,
the arrow points
in the opposite
direction.

The top card shows a half turn to the right.
The bottom card shows a half turn to the left.

12

How are the turns the same?
How are the turns different?

I am turning this card a half turn
to the right.

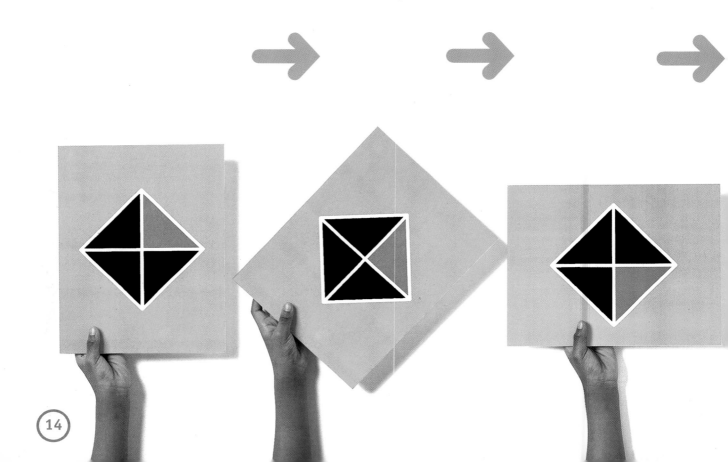

Which card comes next, a or b?

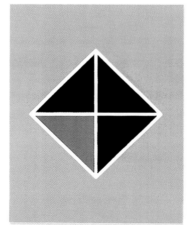

a.

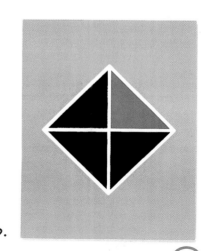

b.

How would this card look
after a half turn?